Artists and Their Art

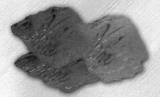

Written by Michael Medearis

STECK-VAUGHN
COMPANY

A Division of Harcourt Brace & Company

www.steck-vaughn.com

CONTENTS

Introduction 3

Chapter 1

Amado Peña 4

Chapter 2

Faith Ringgold 8

Chapter 3

Georgia O'Keeffe 13

Chapter 4

Hale Woodruff 18

Chapter 5

Pablo Picasso.................... 22

Chapter 6

Elisabet Ney 26

You and Your Art 30

Glossary................................ 31

Index.................................. 32

INTRODUCTION

Artists are people who have an ability to see things in a special way and help other people see them, too. Artists are people who are also very talented. They use their talents to create art. The art they create is how they **express** things that they see. Sometimes artists share their art with others. By sharing their art, artists help others see things in a special way.

The six artists described in this book are all very different. They do different kinds of art— some paint, some draw, and some create **sculpture.** Some did a lot of their work in the 1800s, while others are still alive and working today.

But they all have some things in common. They love art, and they all express themselves through their art. Each artist is an interesting person about whom you may enjoy reading. You can see their art in museums around the world.

Chapter 1

AMADO PEÑA (1943–)

Amado Peña

Amado Peña was born in 1943. His mother was Yaqui Indian, and his father was Mexican. Amado Peña began to draw when he was a young boy. He liked to copy comic books. He practiced drawing the figures in the comic books every day. He drew them over and over again until he felt he had a perfect picture. Peña enjoyed working on his art. For him art wasn't work, it was fun.

Peña grew up in Texas. He lived in a city near the Mexican border. His father worked as a firefighter and was a great example to his son.

Peña's father always told him, "No matter what you do, do it the best you can, and the end result can only be good." This made Peña always want to work hard on his art. But when Peña was young, he never thought that he would become a well-known artist.

While Peña was still in high school, he won many art contests. After high school, he went to college. Then he returned to his hometown and became a high school art teacher. He taught art for years. At the same time, he continued to create his own art, too.

Peña loved the art of the **Mestizo** painters. A Mestizo is a person who is part American Indian and part European (Spanish). The paintings of the Mestizo people told wonderful stories about their lives. They were simple paintings that clearly showed the celebrations and work of the Mestizo people.

Many of Peña's paintings show Mestizo people's faces drawn with sharp lines. The faces in these paintings are almost always pointing to the side.

Peña paints in bold bright colors with strong lines. He loves to paint the land and the people of the Southwest. His

Many Peña paintings show Mestizo people.

paintings and prints often show Native Americans and Mexicans doing crafts.

He says, "I thought of the potter creating a work of art from the earth...the weaver creating a blanket. I asked myself, was it enough to just see them...? No, I must paint them, I must draw them, I must record them in some way. So, I did."

Today Peña and his wife live on a ranch in New Mexico. They have a dozen horses. Peña loves to ride on horseback through the canyons. The scenes he sees there are reflected in some of his paintings.

Many of Peña's paintings hang in museums. His posters are often seen in homes, hotels, and offices all over the Southwest. 🖋

←Peña's paintings are bold and bright.

Chapter 2

FAITH RINGGOLD (1930–)

Faith Ringgold

*F*aith Ringgold is an artist who combines paintings and quilts to tell stories. Ringgold was born in New York City. She had asthma as a child, a disease that makes it very hard to breathe. As a child she spent a lot of time in bed. She would write and color and draw and make things out of bits of cloth. She says, "I can't remember a time when I was not doing some form of art."

In school, Ringgold became the class artist. Her teachers often asked her to draw on the blackboard or to create **murals** that told stories about history.

On hot summer nights, Ringgold and her family would climb up to the tar-covered roof of their apartment. They would take blankets, a jug of lemonade, and sandwiches. From the roof, they could see the lights twinkling all over the city. They called the roof "tar beach." This experience would later **inspire** one of Ringgold's art pieces.

Ringgold grew up near City College in New York. She wanted to study art there, but the school would not let women study art unless they were going to be teachers. Ringgold decided that she would teach art to others and still create her own.

Once Ringgold finished college, she visited France and Italy to study painting. She also studied the art of African American painters. After studying paintings of many famous artists, Ringgold became an art teacher.

Ringgold taught and **encouraged** her students to use beads and **fabric** in their art the way African women did. Her students would often ask her why she did not use beads and fabric in her own art.

The questions that her art students asked encouraged her to start working with fabrics. She made sculptures with faces like African masks. She called them "soft sculptures" because they were soft, like giant rag dolls.

Some of her soft sculptures were of people who lived in her neighborhood. Others were of famous people, such as Dr. Martin Luther King, Jr. One soft sculpture was called "The Jones Family." It showed Ringgold, her brother, and her sister with their mother.

Ringgold uses fabric to make her soft sculptures.

When Ringgold was 51, her mother died. She expressed her grief in a new style of art. These paintings had irregular shapes in bright colors. She didn't know what to call them until her husband suggested calling them the Emanon series. *Emanon* is "no name" spelled backwards.

Ringgold sometimes uses bright colors and irregular shapes in her paintings.

Ringgold later changed her style again. She began to make quilted borders for her paintings. Ringgold would write a story about a painting on the quilted borders. Often her stories would follow an African **tradition.** They would tell about a problem, but not the answer. The person looking at the story quilt would have to solve the problem.

One of Ringgold's most famous story quilts is "Tar Beach." This story quilt tells about Ringgold's experiences up on the tar roof of the apartment building where she grew up. This story quilt inspired Ringgold to write and illustrate a children's book.

Today Ringgold is still making her story quilts. Many of her quilts hang in museums.

"Tar Beach" is a story quilt created by Ringgold.

Chapter 3

GEORGIA O'KEEFFE (1887–1986)

Georgia O'Keeffe

Georgia O'Keeffe was born in Wisconsin in 1887. She grew up on her family's farm. O'Keeffe was independent and usually did things her way. Her bold attitude greatly affected her life and her art.

O'Keeffe's mother made sure that her daughters got as much education as possible, including private art lessons. O'Keeffe had a strong interest in art even as a little girl.

When O'Keeffe was in the eighth grade, she announced, "I'm going to be an artist." She later admitted that she did not know exactly where she got the idea but that her mind was made up!

O'Keeffe finished high school and went on to study at famous art schools in Chicago and New York. One day she received a letter from a friend in Texas. A school there needed someone to supervise art classes. O'Keeffe moved to Texas to take the job.

She soon fell in love with the wide-open spaces of the Southwest. She enjoyed taking long walks down country roads. She was fascinated with this sunny, dry land. These **scenic** views were the subject of many of her paintings.

O'Keeffe sent some of her paintings to a friend in New York. The friend showed them to Alfred Stieglitz, a famous photographer who owned an art gallery there. He immediately fell in love with O'Keeffe's work and asked to see more. Stieglitz displayed O'Keeffe's work in his gallery. Later, he fell in love with O'Keeffe herself.

O'Keeffe and Stieglitz were married in 1924. They lived in an apartment with a beautiful view of New York City. There O'Keeffe painted powerful scenes of New York.

During the long winter months in New York, O'Keeffe began to paint very large flowers. These paintings later became very popular. She once said, "Most people in the city rush around, so they have no time to look at a flower. I want them to see it whether they want to or not."

O'Keeffe liked to show the beauty of flowers in her paintings.

O'Keeffe painted landscapes of New Mexico.

During 1928 O'Keeffe went to New Mexico. This trip changed her life forever. When O'Keeffe arrived there she said, "Well! Well! Well!…This is wonderful. No one told me it was like this!"

O'Keeffe loved the land of Northern New Mexico. She found that the thin, dry desert air allowed her to see long distances. Being able to see so far helped O'Keeffe paint some of her most beautiful **landscapes.**

O'Keeffe spent the rest of her life painting scenes of New Mexico. She went back to New York for a few months each year to be with her husband. When he died, O'Keeffe moved to New Mexico to stay. She called it "the most wonderful place in the world."

O'Keeffe would spend hours driving the back roads in New Mexico until she found a scene that looked just right. Then she would stop and paint it.

She especially saw beauty in the bleached bones that lay in the desert. Many of her most famous paintings show white bones against the blue sky and the mountains. Or they show the white bones against the red sands of the desert.

Georgia O'Keeffe lived to be 98 years old. She continued to paint until she died.

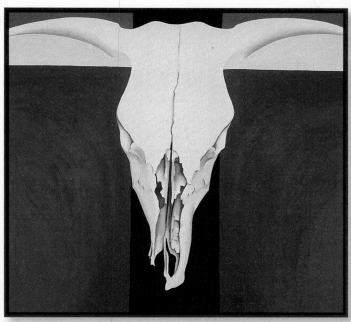

O'Keeffe painted images from the desert.

Chapter 4

HALE WOODRUFF (1900–1980)

Hale Woodruff

*H*ale Woodruff was an African American artist who became an important teacher and leader in fine arts. He was born in 1900 in a small Illinois town. His father died when Woodruff was just a baby. Woodruff and his mother then moved to Nashville, Tennessee, where he grew up. His mother taught him to draw to keep him busy while she worked.

Woodruff had a great talent for drawing. He drew pictures from his family's Bible. He also copied newspaper cartoons. His drawings were so good that he was later chosen to draw cartoons for his high school newspaper.

After finishing high school, Woodruff went to art school. He drew political cartoons and made posters for stores, but he couldn't earn enough money to keep paying for his art classes. So Woodruff had to leave school after four years.

Woodruff wanted to study art in Paris. He knew that he could not afford to go without help. One day he learned about a contest for African American artists. Each winner would get a cash prize. Woodruff entered the contest. He painted three landscapes, one portrait of two women, and a landscape with a figure. This group of five paintings won second prize.

Woodruff painted a landscape for an art contest.

Woodruff received a medal and 100 dollars for his second place prize in the art contest. Then a group of women in a book club gave him an extra 200 dollars to study art in Paris. A newspaper paid him 10 dollars more to create pictures and stories about Paris. Soon he had enough money to go.

Woodruff enjoyed visiting the Paris museums where he saw African art. This art had a great influence on his work. He used West African art styles in his own work. Woodruff also painted pictures that were inspired by African sculptures.

When Woodruff returned to the United States, he became an art teacher in a university. He inspired his students to study and to work hard on their own art. In 1966 Woodruff was given the "Great Teacher" award. This was a great honor. Later, Woodruff wanted to learn about murals, so he went to Mexico and studied with Diego Rivera, a famous Mexican muralist.

Woodruff went on to paint many famous murals. These murals are bold and colorful. Woodruff painted murals to tell the stories of African Americans. He wanted others to understand and see these stories. Woodruff continued working on his art until his death in 1980.

Woodruff painted murals showing the history of African Americans.

Chapter 5

PABLO PICASSO (1881–1973)

Pablo Picasso

*P*ablo Picasso was born in Spain. He was born with an amazing **artistic** talent. He could draw before he could talk. When Picasso did begin to talk, his first word was *pencil.*

One day his father told him to complete a painting of some pigeons. Picasso's pigeons looked just like real pigeons. His father saw that this thirteen-year-old boy had great talent. When Picasso was 14, he became a student at the art school where his father taught.

After Picasso finished school, he shared a **studio** with an artist friend in Spain. They were so poor that Picasso painted chairs and bookcases on the walls to make it look like they had furniture.

Later, Picasso and his artist friend moved to Paris, France. This is where Picasso lived for the rest of his life.

Picasso painted in many styles during his lifetime. He was always willing to try out something new. Picasso believed that an artist could be inspired by, or get good ideas from, the art of other artists. At first, his style looked like the paintings he admired. Then he developed his own style.

When his artist friend died, Picasso was very sad. His painting style changed. He began to paint pictures of sad and lonely people. He used a lot of blue because he thought blue was a sad color. This time of his life was called his Blue Period.

Picasso showed his feelings in his paintings.

Later, Picasso fell in love. During this time, Picasso used a lot of pink and rose colors in his paintings. This was called his Rose Period.

Picasso's style changed again when he saw African art in Paris museums. He liked the way African sculpture stretched and changed body shapes. He also liked the art of African masks.

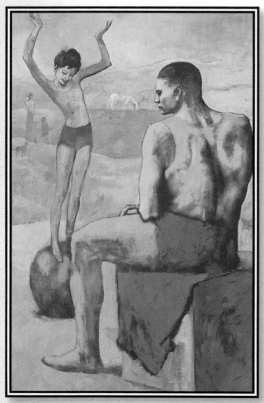

Picasso said the idea for one painting came into his mind the day he first saw African art. In his painting, the bodies look long and flat. Some of the faces look like masks. At the time, many people thought the painting looked strange, and they didn't like it. But now, that painting is called a **masterpiece.**

A painting from Picasso's Rose Period

24

Picasso kept experimenting with shapes as he developed another style. When he painted a person, he tried to show the face looking straight ahead and from the side at the same time. He looked at people and objects and saw them as a combination of simple shapes, such as triangles, cones, and cubes. One writer named this style **cubism.** Picasso said, "I paint objects as I think them, not as I see them."

Picasso lived to be 91 years old, and he continued to be an artist all his life. He made paintings, prints, murals, sculptures, and pottery. He became a very famous artist. Today his art is in museums all over the world.

Picasso's artistic style changed through the years.

Chapter 6

ELISABET NEY (1833–1907)

Elisabet Ney

*E*lisabet Ney was a famous **sculptor.** She was born in Germany in 1833. At that time, girls were treated much differently than they are today. They had to learn to cook, clean, and sew. They were expected to stay with their mothers in the kitchen. They did not get much education.

Ney was a very independent and creative person. She created and designed her own clothes. Sometimes other children laughed at her because her clothes were so different, but Ney wore her creations proudly.

Ney's father was a carver. He carved things from stone. Ney loved spending her free time watching him. Ney learned how to carve in stone from her father.

When Ney was 17, she decided that she wanted to become a sculptor. In the 1800s most art schools did not admit women. Also Ney's parents refused to let her go to art school. But these things did not stop Ney. In fact, she was so **determined** to go to art school that she stopped eating. Finally, her parents gave in.

Ney was allowed to go to Munich, Germany, to study art. There, she became the first woman at the Munich Academy of Art to study sculpture. While at school, Ney sculpted many famous people in Europe, including several kings.

In 1863 Ney married a doctor named Edmund Montgomery. They moved to the United States. They lived in Georgia for a short time before moving to Texas. For the next twenty years, Ney stopped sculpting and spent most of her time caring for her family.

Ney carved this statue from stone.

Then in the early 1890s, Ney was asked to sculpt some early Texas heroes for display at the World's Fair in Chicago. One of those Texas heroes was Sam Houston, the state's first governor.

Ney sculpted many works in her lifetime. Her sculptures include many important Texas governors, university presidents, and her friends.

Elisabet Ney helped change the way people think about art. She helped inspire a school of fine arts at the University of Texas. She even offered to teach students for free.

After Ney's death in 1907, her friends continued to work to fulfill her dreams. They turned Ney's studio into a museum and created many other museums and art centers around Texas. Today people can still visit the Elisabet Ney Museum in Austin, Texas, to see her works.

Ney's studio is now a museum.

You and Your Art

*I*n this book, you have read about six great artists. Some of them lived long ago. Some are alive today. Some of the artists are women, and others are men. Each is known for his or her special style or method of creating art. But in one way all of these artists are the same. Each one found a special way to express himself or herself through art.

The artists in this book began experimenting with art at a young age. You can, too. Look around you. Ideas for wonderful artwork are everywhere if you try to look at things as an artist does.

Think about types of art that interest you. Are they paintings, sculptures, sketches, or pottery? Whatever the type, think about something important to you or something you really like. Then think about a way to express that in art. The possibilities are endless. When you are done, you will have a special piece of art that tells something about you.

Glossary

artistic   having the skills and talent to create art

cubism   a style of art that uses lines, squares, cones, cubes, and triangles to represent real objects

determined   being firm and strong about doing something

encourage   to help or give courage to

express   to show or tell something

fabric   cloth

inspire   to influence the thoughts and feelings of others

landscape   a view of scenery on land

masterpiece   a work that is considered great

Mestizo   the name for a person who is both American Indian and European (Spanish)

mural   a large painting that is done on a wall

scenic   dramatic or beautiful

sculptor   a person who carves wood or stone or shapes clay

sculpture   a statue made of wood, stone, or clay

studio   a place where an artist works on his or her art

tradition   a way of doing things over a long time

INDEX

cubism 25

Mestizo 5, 6, 7

mural 8, 20–21, 25

Ney, Elisabet 26–29

O'Keeffe, Georgia 13–17

Peña, Amado 4–7

Picasso, Pablo 22–25

Ringgold, Faith 8–12

sculpture 3, 10, 20, 24, 25, 27–29, 30

soft sculpture 10

story quilt 12

Woodruff, Hale 18–21